What's Orange?

ORANGE

BALLOON

How many legs does an octopus have?

OCTOPUS

PUMPKIN

FOX

FIRE

What's Yellow?

SUN

DIGGER

SANDCASTLE

Which flowers did
the bee land on?

CHICK

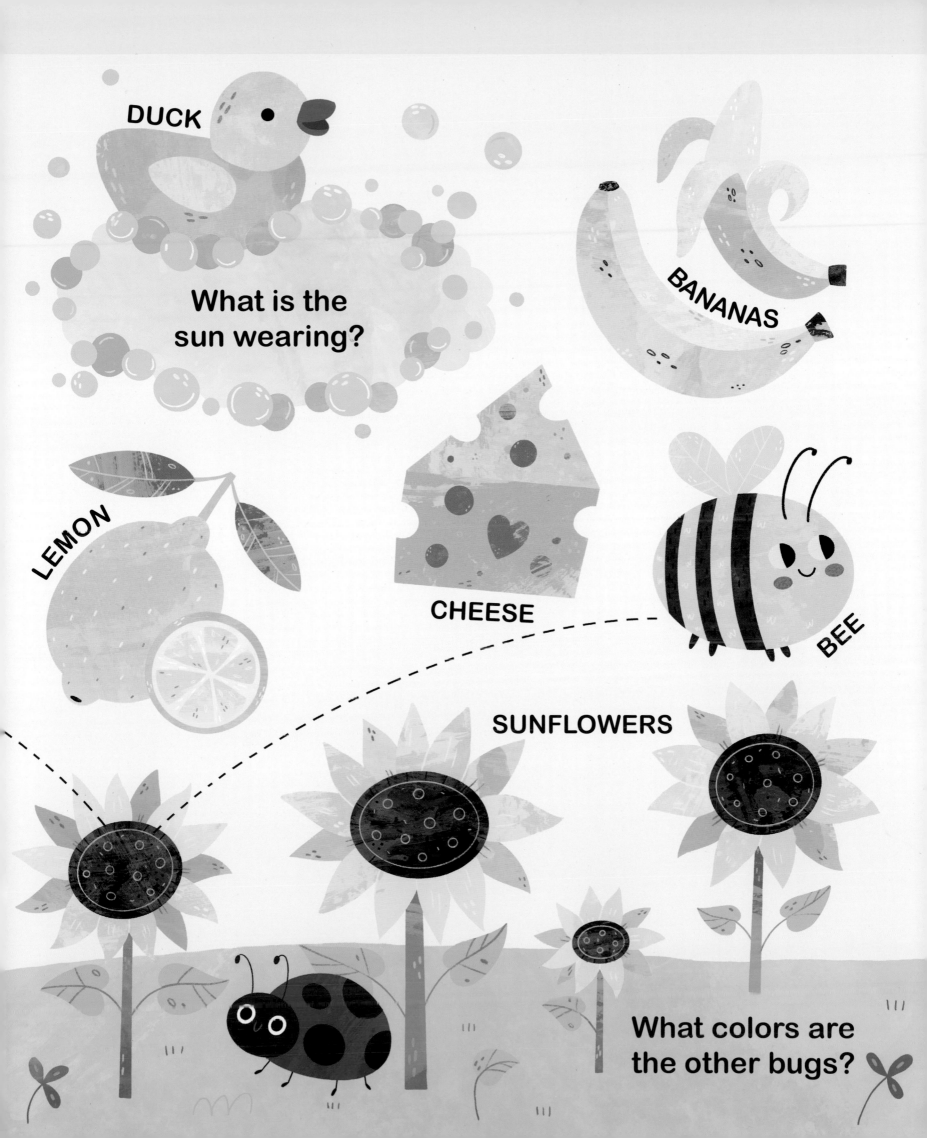

DUCK

BANANAS

What is the sun wearing?

LEMON

CHEESE

BEE

SUNFLOWERS

What colors are the other bugs?

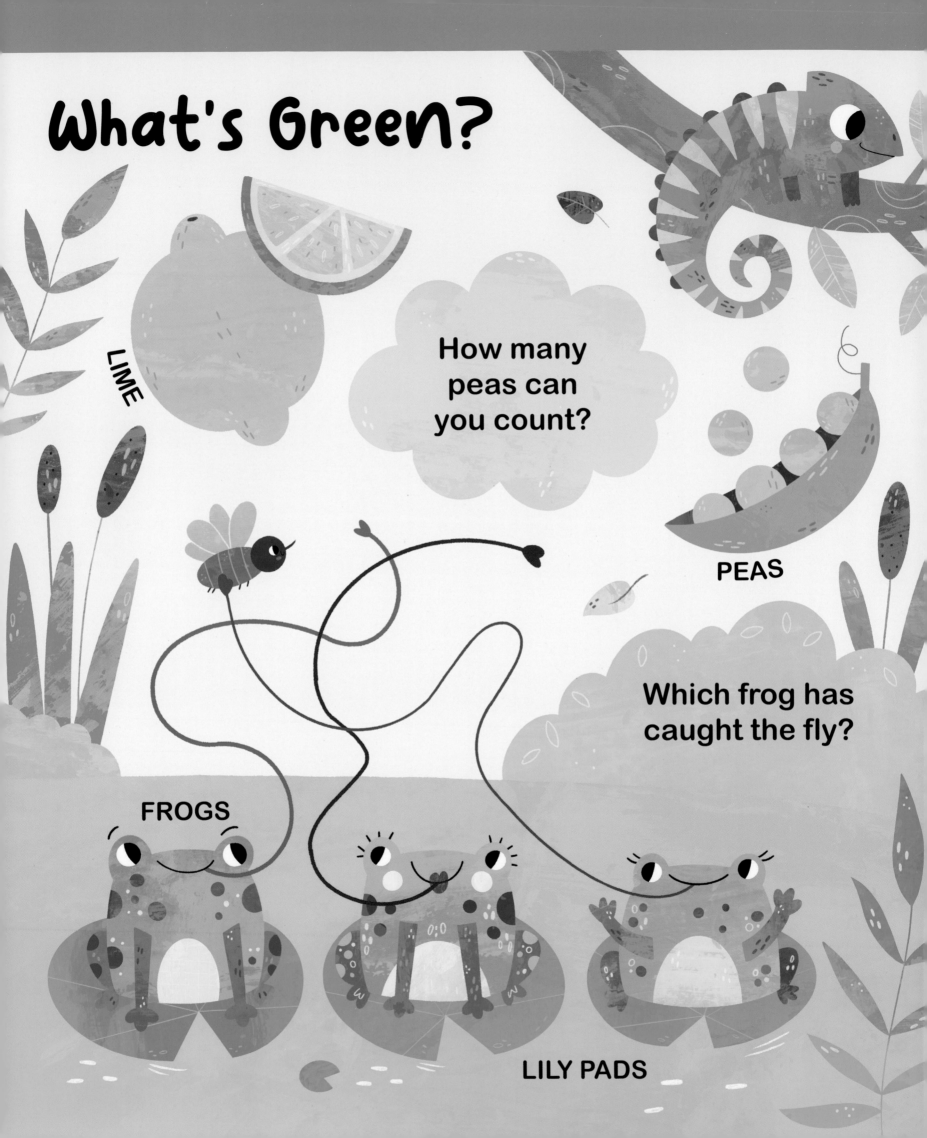

SNAKE

What color are the
snake's spots?

CABBAGE

TREE

DRAGONFLY

TURTLE

CROCODILE

What's Blue?

Which animal is the biggest?

RAIN

BOOTS

UMBRELLA

WHALE

SEA

BLUEBIRD

What would you wear to keep yourself dry?

PANTS

RAINCOAT

BOAT

DOLPHIN

How many fish can you count?

FISH

What's Purple?

GRAPES

BEETLE

T-SHIRT

DRAGON

Can you spot the hidden worm?

EGGPLANT

SOCKS

Who is wearing the other spotted sock?

PLUM

LAVENDER

How many bees can you count?

PENCIL

PERFUME

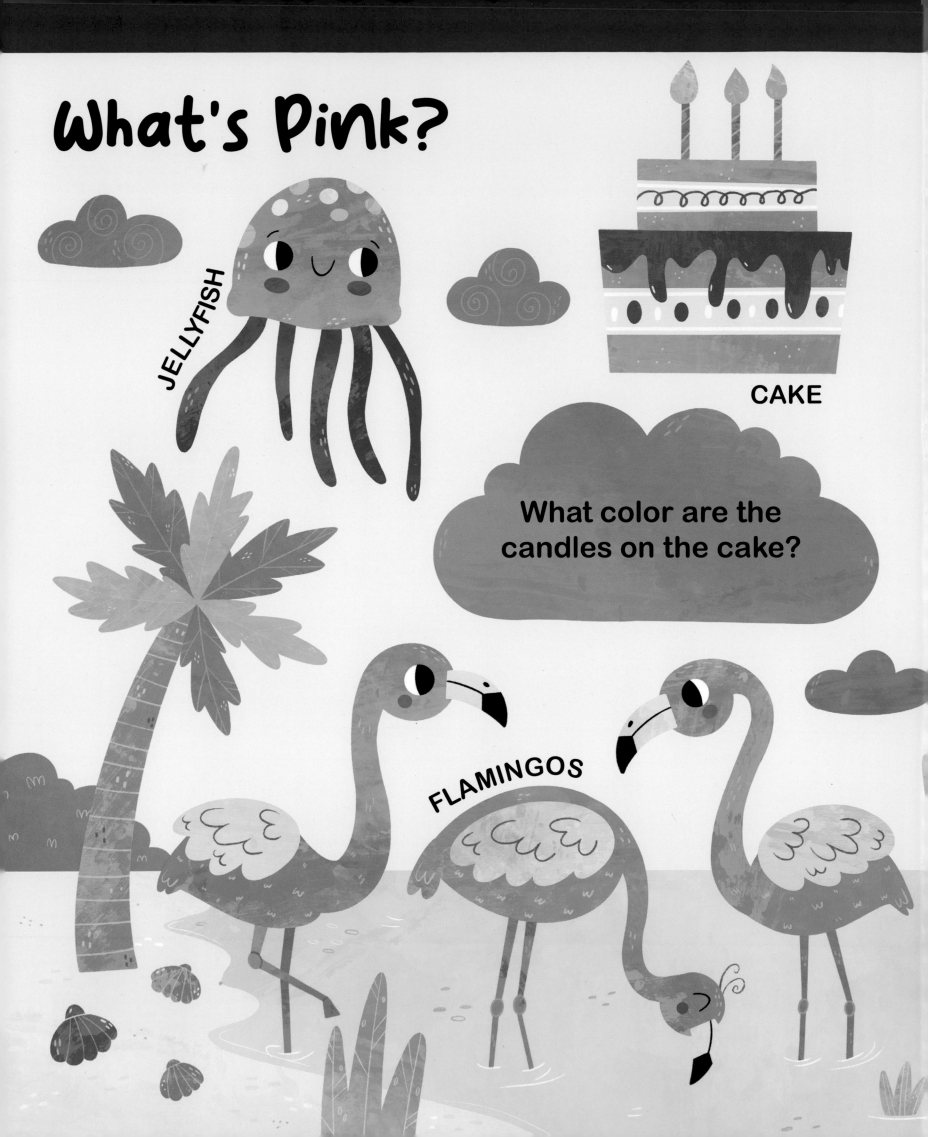

What's Pink?

JELLYFISH

CAKE

What color are the candles on the cake?

FLAMINGOS

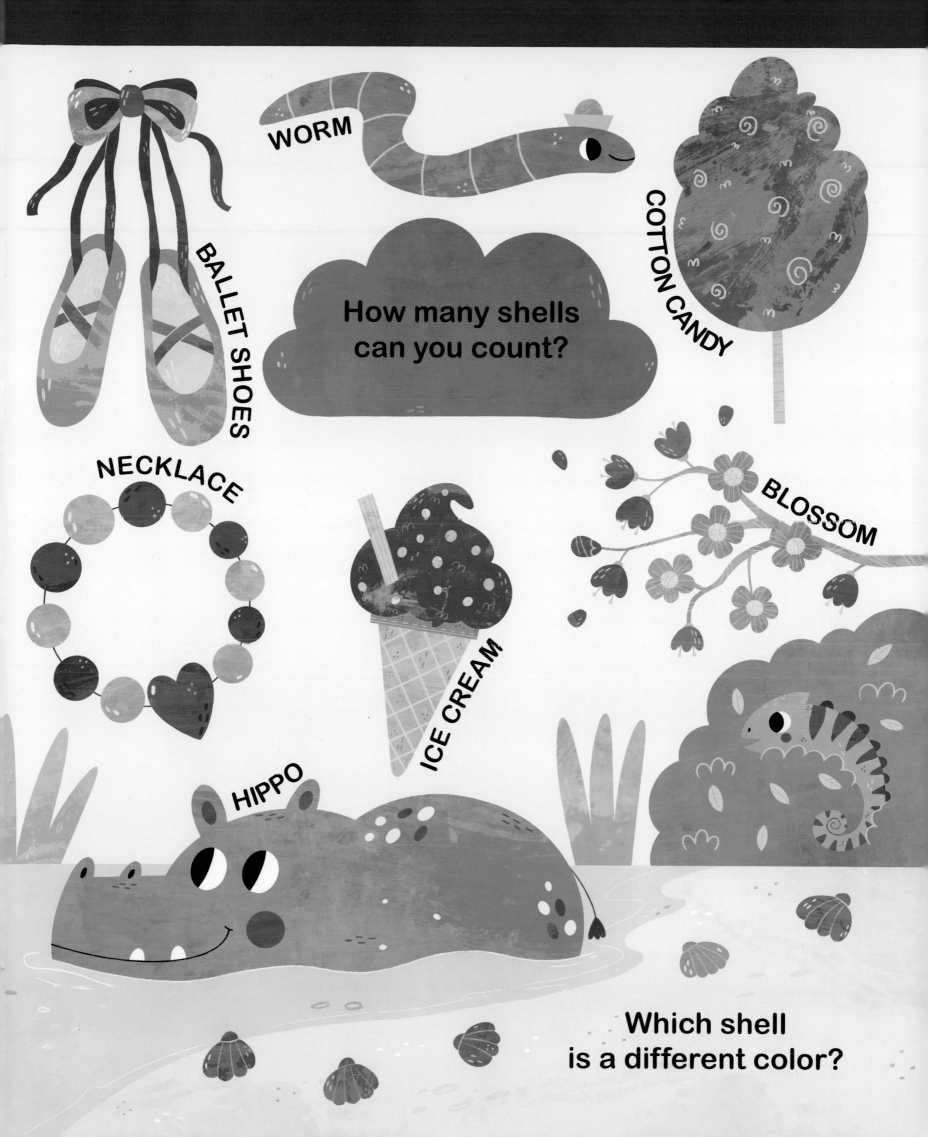

WORM

COTTON CANDY

BALLET SHOES

How many shells can you count?

NECKLACE

BLOSSOM

ICE CREAM

HIPPO

Which shell is a different color?

What's Brown?

DEER

BEAVER

CHAIR

MUSHROOM

How many legs does the chair have?

MUD

BEAR

MONKEY

CHOCOLATE

COOKIES

HORSE

What noise does a monkey make?

Can you spot two differences between the cookies?

What's Gray?

ELEPHANT

ROBOT

STONES

Follow the stepping stones to help the baby elephant find its mom.

KOALA

WOLF

What noise does a wolf make?

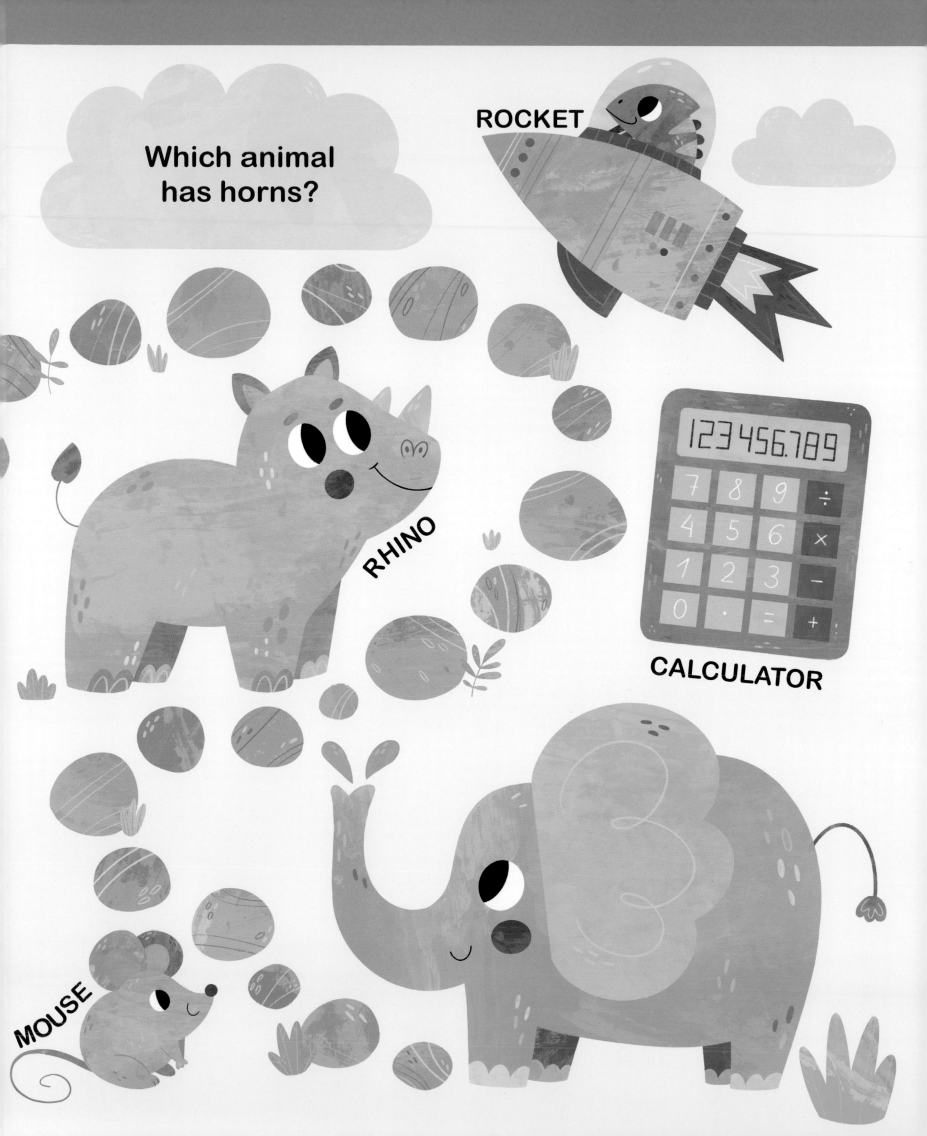

What's Black?

Can you get through the spiderweb maze?

BATS

How many legs does a spider have?

SPIDER

HAT

What colors are the bats' bellies?

CAT

CAULDRON

What's White?

CLOUD

MOON

STARS

SWAN

How many yellow stars can you count?

POLAR BEAR

SNOW

What's MultiColored?

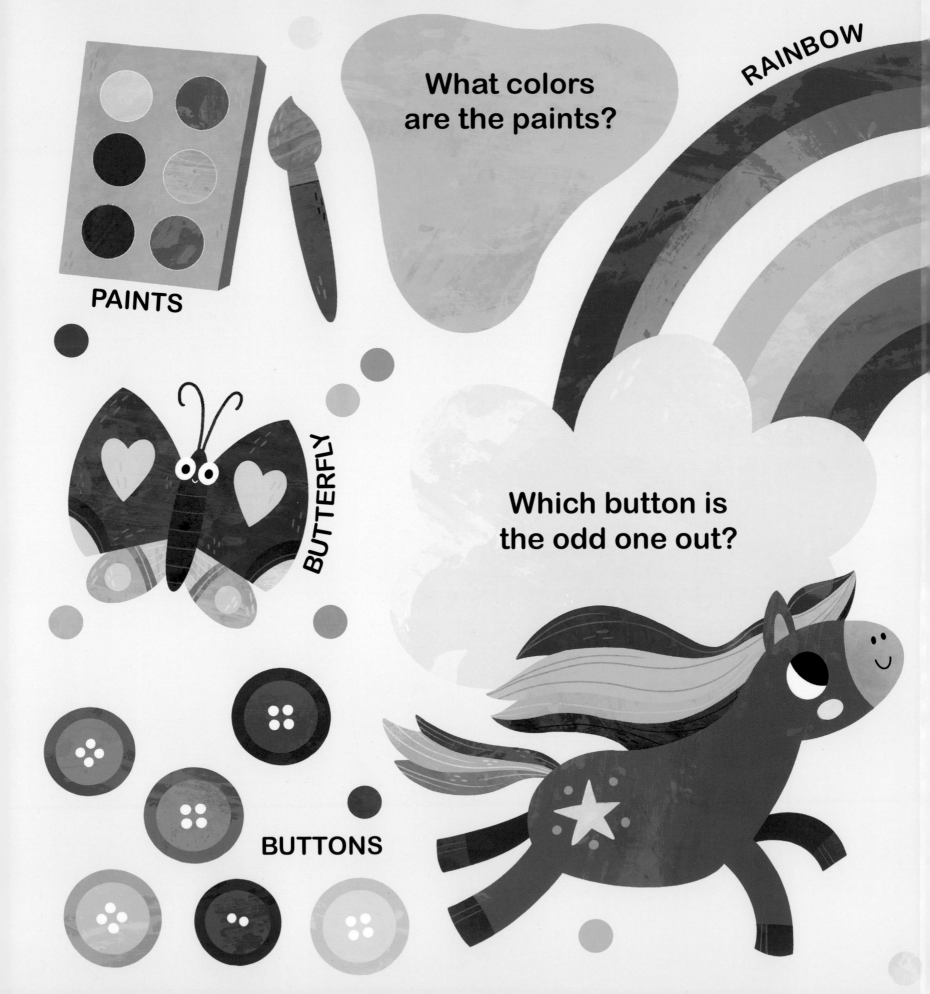

PAINTS

RAINBOW

What colors
are the paints?

BUTTERFLY

Which button is
the odd one out?

BUTTONS